I0486959

Indie

Empowerment

Publishing

Series

by FREE PRESS Publications

© 2 0 0 9

FREE PRESS
A-Listing The Indies

Indie Empowerment Publishing Series

Three-Pack Publishing Kit

3 Speed-Guides from

FREE PRESS Publications

"UNDERWORKED & OVERPAID!
The Indie Author's Freedom
from Nine-to-Five Guide"

and

"OUT STANDING IN THE FIELD:
The Indie Author's Two-Step Guide to
Publishing in Amazon's Kindle Store"

Plus

"QUICK-TIPS FOR PAPERBACKS"
Print Formatting Tips—for *FREE*

3

THREE GUIDES IN ONE:

"UNDERWORKED & OVERPAID!
The Indie Author's Freedom
from Nine-To-Five Guide"
and
"OUT STANDING IN THE FIELD
The Indie Author's Two-Step Guide
To Publishing In The Kindle Store"
Plus
"QUICK-TIPS FOR PAPERBACKS"
~ Bonus Guide ~

ISBN: 1438293461
9781438293462
©2009 All Rights Reserved
by FREE PRESS Publications
Art and Design ©2009
All Rights Reserved

Three Guides in One

UNDERworked and OVERpaid!
The Indie Author's FREEDOM from Nine-To-Five GUIDE

3

Maximize Your E-book
Sales on Amazon.com

OUT STANDING IN THE FIELD
The Indie Author's Two-Step Guide
To Publishing in the Kindle Store

Start earning royalties today!

It's easy

Shortcut

Quick-Tips
FOR PAPERBACKS

Formatting Your
E-Books to Print

Shortcut

Greetings from FREE PRESS!

We thank you for adding our **"Indie Empowerment Publishing Series"** Speed-Guides and Workbooks to your library. In them, you'll find innovative and totally free strategies for maximizing your e-book sales via Amazon.com, for publishing a book in the Kindle Store *on the very first upload*, and for easily formatting your manuscript into a quality paperback edition.

That's three offers in one—enjoy!

C O N T E N T S :

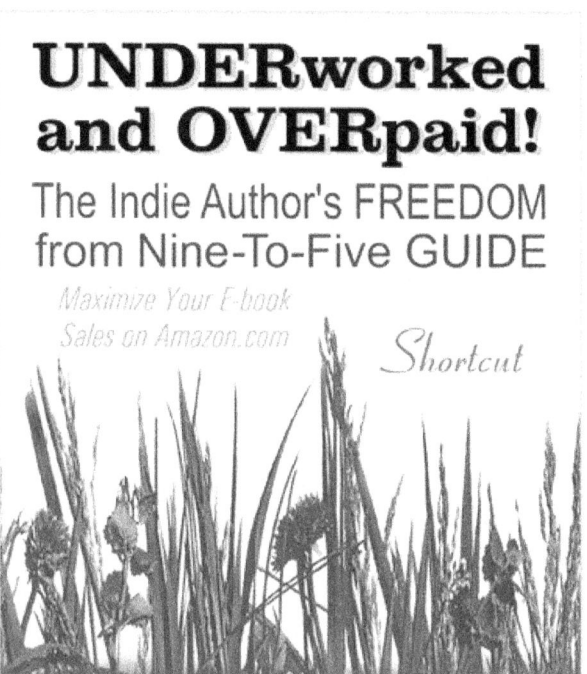

UNDERworked and OVERpaid!

The Indie Author's FREEDOM from Nine-To-Five GUIDE

Maximize Your E-book Sales on Amazon.com *Shortcut*

Kindle Edition: ASIN B002NU5K8C

IES WORKBOOK #1

Write in it, highlight it, dog-ear it—
WE DON'T MIND.

This Guide Contains:

THE TOP TEN MARKETING STRATEGIES TO MAXIMIZING YOUR E-BOOK SALES ON AMAZON.COM...

THAT WON'T COST YOU A DIME

PLUS TEN BONUS TIPS TO INCREASE YOUR TITLES' 'DISCOVERABILITY' ON AMAZON'S BROWSE TREE

Why Publish for Kindle?

"Because, with a thirty-five percent royalty per sale (which no traditional venue can even come close to), and a suddenly booming e-book marketplace, that's where the money is!"

(Excerpt from our Kindle Publishing Shortcut guide, *"OUT STANDING IN THE FIELD: The Indie Author's Two-Step Guide To Publishing in the Kindle Store"*)

INTRODUCTION

Congratulations. You finally did it. You published your book in Amazon's Kindle Store! You're even selling copies of it on a regular basis and you may have already received some favorable customer reviews as well.

Nice job.

As a writer—a published author—it's an encouraging and exhilarating experience watching those sales start to tally up in your royalty account, but now that your feet are wet, you're wondering what you might do to sell even more e-books on Amazon. Perhaps you're even contemplating shelling out some serious dough for a marketing campaign designed to boost your visibility and sales.

Mass e-mailing, publicity packages, press release services, color brochures, a website address…the works.

Of course, by now, however, you couldn't help but notice that the scales seem to tip in favor of the large, mainstream publishing houses listing their titles with Amazon, some very deep pockets that you're required to compete against for a share of the profits in the Kindle Store. You're no fool, so you realize that whatever you're willing to invest in your new project, there's just no way you could ever outspend the big guys.

But did you know that you really don't have to…?

1.
FREE = $ALES

FREE EQUALS SALES
Making Money The Old-fashioned Way

Despite the current buzz about this "new" and daring concept of "free" merchandising, the idea of giving something away in order to generate a ton of sales in return is not a new one by any means. From fast-food to air-fares, from hair-spray to blue-jeans, ever since people began selling things, they've promoted their products and services through the tried-and-true technique of *sampling*, building their businesses, their brands, their customer-base, their product loyalty, AND THEIR PROFITS, in the process.

And you can, too.

Sounds good, but you're an Indie, you counter, so Amazon won't allow you to price your Kindle book below .99 cents...

No they won't—they only give away or discount the major mainstream publishers' titles right now—and there are three solid retail principles at play here which are responsible for this policy, and which you need to fully acquaint yourself with:

1. Only discount what isn't selling;
2. Only give away what isn't selling;
3. Always ask full price for items in demand.

Once in awhile retailers will also implement giveaways to "introduce" brand new items they're adding, or considering adding, to their product line. It would be wonderful to see Amazon doing something similar to this for Indie titles that break through the glass ceiling and, against all odds, consistently hold their own at or above an average sales rank of 15,000 or so. A merit system like this one would ultimately benefit everyone concerned, Amazon, its customers, and independently published authors alike.

But we're not quite there yet so, until then, you, and you alone, are in charge of promoting yourself in the Kindle Store.

Let's get started today:

You can't give away your book on Amazon, but you can, however, still offer your novel or choice excerpts of it for free elsewhere on the web and, while you're at it, run some .99 cent specials from time to time on Amazon, too. Naturally, no promotion is more appealing to shoppers than a *free* one, but take heart in knowing that more and more Kindle owners are becoming aware of the pricing restriction on Indie authors' titles and, as a result, they're more tolerant of the fact that the Indies can't offer them freebies in the Kindle Store. In short, if you're willing to slash your MSRP (Manufacturer's Suggested Retail Price) to the rock bottom price allowable, the majority of Kindle Store customers will fully comprehend that you are trying to *give away* your book to them but that you're being prevented from doing so, and they will positively respond to your generous promotion.

And, although you can't provide active links there, the best place to advertise where your readers can find your free reads is right on your book's detail page, so make certain you list those web-sites, including your own if you have one, in your product's description, or that, if necessary, you modify that description to add them. You might also consider including these same addresses within your Kindle book itself, perhaps even on the title or credits page.

Section six of this first guide provides additional instructions on how to maximize your product detail page to make it sell more books for you. You'll also find a list there of some of the best free web-sites where you can publish your e-book and give it away for free, too.

2.
TWOFERS

TWO-FOR-ONE SPECIALS
The Next Best Thing To Free

As Amazon recently learned with a glut of major publishers' Kindle freebies, there's a limit to how much free stuff you can actually offer in your store before it starts to undermine its viability, especially when freebies aren't actually free to you.

Rule number one: Don't give the store away!

Obvious, huh? But the conundrum here is that, no matter how cumbersome FREE can become for an enterprising shopkeeper, the idea of getting something for nothing <u>never</u> gets old to the buying public. And, of course, it also increases traffic to your storefront tremendously. The perfect compromise then, for retailers who find themselves in this no-win situation, is always that old reliable "Buy One/Get One Free" promotion, which is, after all, the next best thing to giving something away and, arguably, even superior, from a merchant's point of view.

So what do you have that you can give to your customers besides your Kindle book itself?

In addition to that novel, you've probably got some short fiction pieces tucked away somewhere in the closet, or collecting dust up there on the top shelf in your den. Now is the perfect time to polish up those heirlooms and gems and start putting them to work for you:

Pairing one of your short stories with your book FOR FREE entails reformatting your original document to include that freebie at the end of it and then re-uploading and re-publishing the new-and-improved document, as well as modifying your product's title so that customers are aware <u>at a glance</u> of the bargain you're offering them. Alternately, you may just list the twofer special as a separate new title, but either way you'll have to reformat. This strategy may, at first blush, strike you as a somewhat tedious approach to e-book marketing, but you'll soon see that it's worth the effort, because doing so adds a "perceived" *extra* value to your already reasonably priced listing, and giving your readers a twofer deal every now and then will boost your Kindle book's sales without you having to sacrifice one single penny!

3.
JUDGE
THAT
COVER

PEOPLE DO JUDGE A BOOK BY ITS COVER–UNFORTUNATELY

Whether shopping in actual brick-and-mortar stores or perusing virtual catalogs online in their jammies, consumers make a myriad of split-second determinations about the products they are about to buy—or don't buy—based on those products' *appearance*, as well as their affordability, and, in either case, most items they view are so heavily packaged today that shoppers are forced to rely on that packaging alone to evaluate the quality of the contents inside. In fact, as more and more people trend toward making their purchases from online retail and distribution sites, even decisions now about how well-made an article of clothing is, or how good something will taste, rests entirely on the art and design of the web-site and its master, or upon the reputation of the manufacturer, whether good or bad. So, whoever it was who told us long ago that "you can't judge a book by it's cover" however well-meaning their intent might have been in offering such words of solace, was very seriously mistaken. People these days are well-trained as consumers to rapidly and expertly judge your product by its package design and, because of that, an excellent cover on an excellent book can even become a "brand."

But you're not an artist or an illustrator or a graphic designer or…

You don't have to be!

Although most people think of their cameras now as mere toys, technology they take for granted that comes in handy at family picnics or vacations in Disneyland, a camera is a professional design tool. You can make art with a camera. Great art. And you can make money off your art, too.

If your camera is a manual one, be picky when selecting the final image you intend to use. Choose one that's in focus, uncluttered and visually stimulating. If you're planning on using a portrait, take a whole roll of photographs (at least) and proof each of them for "red-eye" or for objects in the background (like trees) that make it ridiculously appear as if something is sprouting out of your model's head. If your novel is of historical subject matter and your heart is set on wrapping it in a classic landscape, be sure that there's no electric wires or jet plumes in the skies, or that there's no modern automobiles looming on the horizon, and the like. These sights are so familiar to us that often we don't even notice that they're there until someone chides us for our gaff. After you've decided on a perfect image, then use a scanner to upload it into your computer for finishing.

Chances are, however, that your camera's a digital one, which means, unless you accidentally hit the 'delete' button (which has been known to happen now and then) you really can't go wrong with any of your photographs. Just aim and shoot and, voila, you've got dozens of masterpieces to choose from. Or at least one nice image you can then upload to your computer and start playing around with.

And, if you've got a digital camera or a photo scanner, then you probably have a computer design program as well, even though you may be unfamiliar with how to employ it to its full potential. Be this PhotoShop® or Paint® or something similar, it behooves you now, as an independent publisher, to consult that 'Help' menu tab in order to learn some of the basic principles of your design program so that you'll be able to enhance, crop, re-size, add type, and remake your photographs into eye-catching cover art. You'll profit from this knowledge so learn-while-you-earn and start designing. It's also a lot of fun once you get the hang of it!

NOTE: If you do not size and format your cover correctly, it can fail to upload, or, alternately, be removed by Amazon for failing to meet its criteria. For specific Kindle image formatting guidelines and other tips for successfully adding a finished cover (and manuscript) on the first upload, consult the second guide in this workbook series, *OUT STANDING IN THE FIELD,* our publishing shortcut. It offers a fail-safe publishing approach for Kindle's Digital Text Platform publishers. You'll find lots of valuable post-publishing tips in it as well.

4.
T0PYGARF!KLE ERRS

TYPOGRAPHICAL ERRORS
Why Spell-Check is Your Friend

To be blunt, it really doesn't matter how slick you make your book cover if it's only concealing a defective product within, which for a book typically translates into a lot of bad grammar, misspellings, inexplicable punctuation, etceteras. The bottom line is that producing a quality product, both inside and out, gives you a significant competitive and marketing advantage, so if you're going to spend money on anything to advance your e-book enterprise, then spend it for some professional editing, because a poorly edited book is not only the mark of an amateur, it's insufferable, and completely antithetical to generating sales. Keep in mind, too, that as an Indie you're up against some serious heavy-hitters, big publishing houses and their famous top selling authors, so put your best foot forward right away, because your readers will not give you a second chance if your novel is so riddled with typos and the like that it's just plain unreadable. In fact, you'll lose whatever money you do make on those initial sales because customers will most assuredly return your defective e-book for a refund, and maybe even complain about the content to Amazon. It's hard to redeem yourself once that happens.

To avoid unnecessary setbacks like this, examine your finished product/s once again, and this time really scrutinize your work in order to make sure it's as close to perfection as humanly attainable. And, in performing this worthy task, be objective about it, because you're not just an author anymore, you're also a publisher, and an editor, and a merchandiser, and—potentially—a brand-name, too.

NOTE: The following is a good example as to what other kinds of common errors you should be looking for in your manuscript, in addition to those missing or misspelled words, bad grammar, incomplete sentences, or improper punctuation:

"Too" means *also*; "to" means *toward*; "two" means *more than one and less than three*. (Check thoroughly for similar misuses and foibles.)

5.
OPTIMIZING
MAXIMIZES!

OPTIMIZE YOUR E-BOOKS
TO MAXIMIZE YOUR SALES
(Or: Is there life after Kindle?)

All e-reading devices are not created equal! And neither are all e-books.

That is to say, despite the major achievement of successfully converting your novel into a digital edition, if you've only formatted it to be read on the Kindle, then you're losing out on sales.

The e-book and e-reader marketplace, although still emerging, is thriving now, yet currently Amazon only facilitates the sale and downloading of Kindle books to two other e-reading models besides its Kindle wireless reader: Iphone and Ipod Touch. This limits your earning potential considerably because there are a great many more e-readers available out there than just these devices, and a host of others still in the works.

As to electronic books themselves, Kindle Mobi, PDF, RTF, Epub, LRF, Plain Text, PDB, Online HTML, Javascript…there are also a lot more e-book styles that your novel can be and should be available in.

To be sure, publishing for Amazon's Kindle was a smart move on your part, because Amazon *sells*, and their Kindle distinguishes itself from the pack with its unique Text-to-Speech feature which gives a Kindle edition the added appeal of a pseudo-audio book, but this extra is offset by the fact that Kindle books are digitally restricted media, so they can't be easily shared or read on the majority of other wireless devices. Moreover, while there are still even more nifty things that a Kindle wireless can do that most others cannot, the reality is that many book lovers simply want to *read* their e-books and do so without all those bells and whistles, whether by means of a hand-held device or even online with their computers. To reach that market as well, you'll need to make your e-book accessible to them, which means reformatting it more universally, *optimizing* it so everyone can download and read it in any format.

In the world of electronic publishing, the easiest and most optimal document for conversion to e-books is Microsoft Word or Microsoft Rich Text Format.

We've already written the publisher's shortcut bible on this subject so, since this guide here is concerned with the aspects of free marketing, we'll avoid being redundant in it. However, if you did read and utilize our shortcut, then you already know that Amazon's Digital Text Platform can beautifully translate these types of documents without a single hitch, and so can the other e-publishing channels we've just listed.

From a financial perspective, it's more than worth it to take the time to figure out how to optimize your documents so they'll flow freely and as nicely as possible on all the other e-reading devices in the market. It won't cost you anything to do this and it'll triple your sales—at least.

6.
LOCATION LOCATION LOCATION

LOCATING YOUR ADS IN ALL THE RIGHT PLACES

It's an old expression but it still holds true, "location, location, location," is one of your greatest assets, and, even though the Internet has helped enormously to level the playing field for the little guy, where a business is located on the web is as critical as ever to the success of the enterprise.

As we've mentioned before, there are a lot of other places online where you can publish and sell your e-book/s, and you should sign on with them ASAP, but, undeniably, the hottest spot at the moment is Amazon's Kindle Store. Guarantee you, that's where you'll generate more than 90% of your e-book sales.

For real, the sky's the limit in the Kindle Store—you can make 90% of a little or 90% of a lot, depending on your marketing savvy and presentation skills, so it deserves the lion's share of your marketing attention. Start with your e-book's detail page, which, with its "Also Bought" and "Sales Percentage" sections, currently reads as an advertisement for other authors' titles. Here's how to begin to reclaim this page as your own:

1. Is your title attention-grabbing? You've only got seconds to hook your customer so it has to be compelling. Also does it tell them enough? Remember, you can put a ton of info in that title space so don't waste the opportunity to speak there. Just be tasteful with what you say, and make sure to spell everything right, while you're at it!

2. Does your book have a cover image? If so, is it an eye-catching one? Crisp? The title legible? If your book's on special this week or month, does it clearly say that at a glance?

3. How's the description? Is it a decent-length good synopsis, without any typos? You've got up to 4000 characters you can use in this box in order to pique people's interest and make a sale. That's a lot! In it you can also include your bio and some of your freebie web addresses, too. Anything whatsoever that's relevant to you and your novel.

4. Is your MSRP competitive? As we've said, you don't necessarily need a discount to sell your Kindle book, but it absolutely must be reasonably priced or you won't be able to move it off your shelves.

5. How about categories? You're allowed up to five of them you know. When your e-book takes off and you don't have categories listed, or not enough of them, then you're excluding your title from appearing

on as many bestselling lists as possible, including Amazon's bestselling "new releases" lists, which you can stay on for weeks at a stretch, if not months. More categories = more bestselling lists = more sales.

6. Keywords are key to your success: In the space provided for keywords fill in as many relevant and common words and phrases as can possibly fit there. This will insure that the book shows up in customer search results *and* appear in all the appropriate places of Amazon's Kindle store with all the other books of its type, including those of famous authors.

(Now click SAVE!)

Okay, so far everything's perfect…you've hooked a customer and now they're going to download their free sample:

1. Is your cover image right smack on the first page of your e-book? Does the synopsis follow immediately after it? If there are customer reviews of your book or of other writings you've published, have you included a good sampling of them on the third or fourth page? Is the credit page clear and concise with no typos? This is all important because sometimes customers don't immediately read their free downloads. If you provide all this information within the first few pages of your e-book, it will refresh their memory when they come back to your sample and

thereby increase the chances considerably that they'll purchase the whole package from you.

2. Have you included a brief thank-you-for-your-patronage blurb in the back of your e-book? (Nice guys can finish *first*, you know, if they try hard enough!) As well, is there a bibliography listed there for your other available titles, and where your customers might find them, and where they can also read you for free…etceteras?

Whether to sell your e-book or to promote it for free, your going to e-publish now in more than just the Kindle Store, so rather than making different editions of the same book for each web-site, take the extra time right now to advertise all the relevant information in one uniform version. There are more and more places springing up for you to sell and promote your e-books in; it won't cost you anything, so consider launching a virtual storefront in any or all of these ones ASAP:

- *Smashwords.com*
- *Lulu.com*
- *Scribd.com*
- *Mobipockets.com*
- *Sony.com* (by the end of 2009)

On these sites, or on any other ones you choose, always provide live links to your Kindle titles because people still prefer to buy from Amazon than from these newer e-store operators. Notwithstanding that truism, however, set up each of your e-stores with the ultimate aim of selling books and making money in them, because you will definitely make some sales on each of these sites, especially if you fill your storefronts with quality e-books and promote them from time to time with freebies. Most importantly right now, these sites will serve as virtual billboards for you, advertising your products, spreading your name across the internet, and driving more and more traffic to your Kindle Store as a result. In the industry, we call that kind of attention "buzz". Buzz is very, *very* good for business. So go out there and get some!

7.
SOCIALIZING
MAXIMIZES!

SOCIAL NETWORKING YOUR WAY TO THE TOP

You've probably heard this more than once in your lifetime but it still bears repeating: You've got to network in business. Rubbing elbows is how it's always been done and always will be, but keep in mind, when you're having a conversation these days, no matter who it's with or how important the topic, if it's taking place off-line, IT DOESN'T REALLY COUNT.

So ignore *Facebook* and *Myspace*, with all their clutter and controversy, if you choose, but don't underestimate the author networking sites like *Authorsden.com* and *RedRoom.com*. They're free to join and, geesh, even Barack Obama has his own *RedRoom* page! Obviously, since you can write as well as the president can, you should go get yourself one, too. Once you set up your author profile account with *Redroom* and get approved by the site administrator as a legitimate author, you can begin to register all of your e-books there as well. They'll then show up on your bio page and in your bibliography page, with direct links to your Amazon pages, including their product images.

Also open an account on *Twitter.com* and start "tweeting" your activities and book links right now.

Then set up a link to your Twitter profile on all your other sites asking your visitors to "Follow Me On Twitter". Remember, your "fans" "friends" and "followers" are your potential customers, too, and, as you accumulate more and more of them, you'll also be developing an invaluable contact list for marketing…all for free.

If you've got some time left on your hands, you might also consider blogging now and then. Don't set up too many of these accounts, however, because blogs that aren't regularly updated with original content will just get ignored. For user-friendly blog-sites that receive a lot of traffic and offer their bloggers every feature under the sun, check out *WordPress.com* and *LiveJournal.com*. By the way, you can also blog from your *Redroom* profile page.

But wait there's more. *Hubpages.com* has taken the art of blogging to an even higher level, merging a writer networking site with the potential to earn royalties from your magazine-styled articles . Profits are earned by participating with *Google's Adsense* program where, ostensibly, you can earn a small percentage of the pay-per-clicks that appear on your hub articles. There are some terrific authors on *Hubpages* and, aside from the earnings potential, which will be nominal, your articles will get a lot of exposure there. It's also a great opportunity to make more fans and friends, especially if you always strive to create totally unique and useful content. Moreover, since you can add an Amazon capsule to each of your hubs, you can list your Kindle books for sale and drive traffic back to your Amazon pages.

Similar to *Hubpages*, is *Triond.com* and *Helium.com*. They differ in that these two sites pay you direct royalties on your original articles. Each is set up and works differently, of course, and the earnings you derive from your membership on them may be marginal, but they offer additional exposure and interaction, nonetheless.

As you can see, the possibilities for socializing on the web are endless. It's all good for business and it's 100% free, so don't be shy about it. Start gabbing and blogging and tweeting and hubbing away!

8.
STOCK
UP

STOCKING YOUR SHELVES
(Or: What Do You Know?)

Variety is indeed the spice of life…and the key to making more sales.

We won't belabor this next point too much because it's more than obvious that if you only have one e-book for sale in your storefront, then, even if your readers went wild over it, you won't be able to generate any repeat customers or build "brand loyalty" for your number one product—YOU.

Simply put, a dearth of choice in your offerings is robbing you of sales.

Now, we fully understand that you can't crank out a quality novel every month of the year, but then nobody says you actually have to do that. Concentrate instead on short pieces of nonfiction, say 5000 words or less, written with authority on a particular subject you know a lot about.

Think hard for a moment on what you're expert at. Be it cooking gourmet meals or collecting rare coins, you know more than you think you do, and there are plenty of people in the world eager to pay you for that knowledge.

FACT: From romance to finance, some of the best-selling books on Amazon, or anywhere for that matter, contain instructional or motivational content. When well-written, informative, and modestly priced, self-improvement guides will not only sell briskly for you on their own but, through a boomerang effect, they'll also help sell your novel, too.

Get writing, stock up those shelves, and sell more books today!

NOTE: Do not endeavor to fill your Kindle storefront with *public domain titles! Effective immediately, Amazon is prohibiting the publishing of such material due to a surplus of them, as well as numerous customer complaints from Kindle owners/victims purchasing these products. For this reason, DTP publishers are now also experiencing inordinate delays in their new titles going live for Kindle (over a week in some cases), including those who are just making minor changes to existing ones already available. Amazon is presently sifting through all new Kindle releases to enforce their NO PUBLIC DOMAIN TITLES ALLOWED policy, so it won't be worth your bother to upload one. Not only will they not publish it, they might even block your DTP account so that you can't publish anything else ever again.

Public domain titles are those whose copyrights have legally expired, such as "Pride and Prejudice" by Jane Austen.

9.
ROTATE YOUR STOCK

ROTATING YOUR E-BOOKS
Keeping Your Inventory "Fresh"

(This technique might only double your sales but, hey, double ain't too bad!)

Inventory is inventory, right? Nothing less and nothing more…?

Well, yes and, on the other hand, *no*:

Every now and then, because you impressed a shopper with the professional presentation of your book's detail page, she'll click on your author name out of curiosity. When she does that—ta dah—every e-book you've published in your Kindle Store shows up. That's great, you think, but in truth it's not too exciting at all, and may even be overwhelming.

And the more titles you add to your Kindle store, the longer your inventory list grows. But, while adding new titles is a good thing, because it helps to revitalize your storefront, it still won't exactly make everything else there look "fresh" will it?

Brick-and-mortar retailers have to go to great expense and great lengths to *freshen* their inventory, periodically rearranging their shelves and regularly rotating stock to give the appearance that all of their merchandise has just arrived. While retailers of e-products (like Kindle books) don't have that kind of overhead, they're still posed with a similar problem in selling them, because, although it's true that e-books don't collect dust or have a shelf-life to speak of, they can still get stale. The concept and practice of "rotating stock" was invented to resolve this problem. Unfortunately, in a virtual store, you can't really shuffle your inventory around!

Or can you…?

DEPARTMENT STORES: What would happen if you added another name right beside your own on some of your publications? What if, for instance, "Click Here For John Doe's Specials" or "Click For All John Doe's Guides" or "Click For John Doe's Short Stories" was your co-author or wrote the introduction to that cookbook you're just about to publish?

Enhancing your shoppers' "shopping experience" by grouping related listings with specific internal links such as those above creates "departments" in your Kindle Store that can easily be visited with just one click. And guess what happens when you do tell people to "click here" in order to view something special? They will!

In short, "Click Here" links not only organize your shelf space, they help to keep things exciting—fresh —and increase the likelihood that a shopper will browse your store longer. Remember, the longer you can keep shoppers browsing, the more products they'll view, and the more products they view, the greater the chances they'll buy something.

NOTE: We urge you to be creative with your "Click Here" links and always incorporate your author name into them because, as is the case with registering domain names or e-mail addresses, the titles of these links must be unique ones. If they're the same as another vendor's then they'll open to their store listing as well. For example, we use "Click For Our Best Prices" so if you accidentally choose that phrase, too, our titles will automatically show up right along side of your designated ones, and that mistake can cost you a sale or two if your customers should decide to buy any of our products instead. Also, be very certain that the links you create in order to group particular items together are_word for word, letter for letter, completely identical. If they're not, then you'll just be scattering your inventory all over the sidewalk, so to speak, and this marketing approach won't work at all.

10.
THE WORKS

WORKING THE FORUM
Discussing Do's and Don'ts

The Internet has brought us so many amazing possibilities—now, not only can we chat with imaginary friends, but we may also fight with imagined enemies!

Having said that, this section contains a couple of important caveats about customer discussion threads and the DTP Publisher forums, which is why we didn't list these under the social networking part of our guide.

YES, participating in discussion boards and forums, especially those all over Amazon's site, can earn you "friends" and generate book sales, BUT done to excess it can also backfire on you, bringing you instant notoriety instead of the acclaim that you deserve. This, you'll discover, will be true whether or not your contributions are helpful and add to the conversation. Also, as in real life, be aware that there are some people who are just plain disagreeable folks, hiding behind their cyber identities and browsing the threads just looking for a fight. Accordingly, proceed cautiously whenever posting your replies on a thread or initiating a brand new topic, and interact sparingly once you do because, if people feel that you're overworking the boards, you'll be quickly considered a spammer and be "ignored" on them, or, even worse, you'll find yourself attacked by a mob. And you don't want that.

As pertains to the DTP publisher "support" forums, an extra word of caution: These threads are indeed intended for the Indie community and in perusing them, you'll discover that there are many questions being posted that you can easily answer in order to assist your colleagues who are experiencing various technical difficulties. Providing assistance is a good thing to do and, now and then, even adding one of your e-book's links to such responses is also prudent, but, for the same reasons as mentioned before, keep this activity to a minimum as well.

ALSO be on high alert for (and avoid like the plague) those DTP publishers who, on the guise of offering help, constantly work the boards day and night for their sales, even customizing their handles so that, whenever they post on a thread or start their own, active links to their various web-sites and book pages *automatically appear*. Knowledgeable or not, these types amount to nothing but professional spammers who think of the forums as their own. Consequently, they'll aggressively "defend" their "turf" from helpful contributors like yourself, whom they may regard as a serious challenge to their hegemony. You won't have to look very hard for these trolls, they'll find you, but you'll recognize them instantly by the number of posts attributed beside their names or handles. Always look there then, and, if you encounter anyone with well over a hundred posts, just ignore them! Eventually they'll have to cease and desist—some of these guys have nearly a thousand such messages, well beyond the threshold number that can result in expulsion, if the matter is brought to the attention of Amazon.

As to minimizing your own participation on these threads: It isn't even necessary to post one hundred times, let alone a thousand, if what you have to say on those occasions when you do speak is insightful and truly helps to solve a problem. By the same token, don't be afraid to post a question yourself if you're having publishing issues. DTP is *very* problematic and its administrators aren't usually around or don't answer soon enough to be helpful. There are lots of your fellow publishers who can and will answer your inquiry or confirm the presence of a sudden DTP glitch so you don't have to feel (or deal) all alone. Ideally, that is what these threads are for.

So make monitoring the discussion boards a part of your regular routine, and even network with those participants who seem cooperative—we do from time to time—but in short, less *is* more when working the public forums for self promotional purposes. Only in this manner will people actually listen and talk to you, and, if you do it right, every single time, some will even *buy* what you're saying!

THE TEN BEST PRACTICES FOR GETTING "DISCOVERED" ON AMAZON

GETTING DISCOVERED
10 Tips For Increasing Your 'Discoverability' on Amazon

The following activities done routinely will make your books appear higher and higher in Amazon customer search results, as well as in Amazon's book recommendations. They're all FREE and they'll help you to sell better, so if you're not doing these things for your titles already then get busy now because, by not taking advantage of these particular site features, you're obscuring your visibility on Amazon and cheating yourself of sales:

1. Tag your titles with the maximum number of common words and phrases that are relevant to them.

2. Submit well-written and concise search suggestions for them.

3. Create "Listmania" lists with them and include major authors' titles on those lists.

4. Create "So-You'd-Like-to" lists with them.

5. Solicit reviews of your e-books from your colleagues, customers, fans, friends, and even your own family members.

6. Write favorable customer reviews of popular books you've read that are similar to yours in subject matter and include <u>one</u> book link in each of them.

7. Vote on customer reviews of your titles, and (every blue moon) even graciously post a short reply to a five-star one that catches your attention.

8. Set up a *complete* AuthorCentral profile on Amazon and blog from it on a fairly regular basis. (Currently only available for authors who have books in print, Amazon just announced that this "new" feature will soon extend to authors with Kindle books, too.)

9. Set up a *complete* customer profile on Amazon so you'll get "noticed" with your reviews, lists, and guides. Be sure to include an active link there to your bestseller in the space furnished for a web-page address. Feel free to also add it as one of your favorite books, too.

10. Proofread anything and everything that you intend to post online for errors of any kind **at least ten times** before posting it anywhere. Don't get sloppy with your public image—nobody buys books from illiterate-sounding writers!

CONCLUSION

The digital era is turning the publishing industry upside down, and savvy Indies like yourself are giving mainstream traditional publishers, who are unwilling to adapt their prices, their production, and their products accordingly, a very serious run for the money. Many of these companies are acting genuinely startled by the emergence of a healthy e-book marketplace, even though the technologies behind it all have been around for practically a decade. Some of these dinosaurs are headed for extinction if they can't make the digital transition. Take *"Readers Digest"* for instance, which just recently filed for Chapter Eleven.

Their loss is your gain!

The large publishing houses have traditionally regarded the matter of e-books with contempt, even with hostility, but this is folly on their part because the e-book is a manufacturer's and retailer's dream come true: a product that exists in virtual reality but doesn't have to be physically manufactured in a plant or stored someplace in a warehouse. Plus you can sell an e-book anywhere, anytime, to anybody. And just how many copies you sell is limitless. Yes, you have to make price concessions for a product that most consumers are aware <u>has no overhead</u> and, yes, you have to invest the time to learn how to create quality e-books with enough flexibility that they can be downloaded and read on any electronic reading device. But guess what? That's how you make money in publishing these days!

As to spending big bucks to attract customers, that old "money makes money" theory just isn't true anymore in this the age of the Internet. *Sales makes sales makes money*, and you can generate them without spending a dime if you know a few good tricks.

With that goal in mind, we hope you will undertake right now to implement the free marketing ideas we have compiled in this guide, and start selling more of your e-books today.

Oh, and we'd be remiss if we didn't also add...

Good luck with your books!

OUT STANDING IN THE FIELD
The Indie Author's Two-Step Guide
To Publishing in the Kindle Store

Start earning royalties today!

it's easy

get published in hours

Shortcut

Kindle Edition: ASIN B002ECFQM4

To prove our point that you don't need to be a technological wiz kid or have a state-of-the-art computer system and sophisticated programs in order to get your work in Amazon's Kindle Store TODAY, we published this guide for Kindle using only *Windows-95* and a *Dial-up* Internet connection.

That's right, *Windows-95* and *Dial-up*!

(So what are you waiting for?)

1.

Log in…

2.

Upload...

YoU'Re pUbLiShed!

INTRODUCTION

You've got the great American novel languishing there in a folder on your computer and you've been browsing the Kindle Store for days now, if not weeks, searching for a *simple* how-to guide so you can publish it. You've looked at so many manuals by now that your head's spinning and you're totally discouraged—all of them chock full of Kindle-speak, complicated code, caveats, and priced astronomically.

DON'T GIVE UP! The truth is that, despite the impression those expensive and needlessly complex instruction manuals give, Amazon's created a fairly accessible platform to work with and you really don't need very many skills to publish yourself in the Kindle Store.

Why should independent publishers and authors publish their work for Kindle? Because, with a thirty-five percent royalty per sale (which no traditional venue can even come close to) and a suddenly booming e-book marketplace, that's where the money is! Moreover, Amazon desperately wants your titles to stock its practically empty bookshelves with, and it needs them in order to successfully compete against, and ultimately dominate, the other e-book retailers who presently have more offerings. That's why Amazon-Kindle is actively wooing the Indies, because they know that if they can't get more books in their Kindle Store <u>right now</u>, then they'll be quickly overtaken by the growing ranks of new e-book enterprises out there intent on taking a chunk out of Amazon's earnings and who are already skillfully undermining their profits, as we speak.

ELECTRONIC PUBLISHING: Face it, regardless of whether we personally prefer paperbacks and hard-covers over electronic books, Amazon's wireless reader, despite it's alleged defects, is enormously popular right now. Even Oprah has one and she "loves it" she recently announced to her audiences. And, with only 300,000+ books available at the moment for the ever burgeoning mass of Kindle owners, there's an overwhelming and unprecedented need in the Kindle Store for fresh, new material, which the lumbering publishing giants, with their long-standing disdain of e-books, stale back-lists, and their tedious publishing methods in general, simply cannot or will not furnish.

That spells a lot of opportunity for those Independents who can *literally* "move on a dime" and still provide quality e-books for a hungry readership, which, guessing from the rather steep price of the Kindle, also has a lot of disposable income on hand.

Sounds good, huh?

It is good, but "quality" is the operative word here, because the Kindle clan is basically no different than regular book-buyers in terms of what they're looking for when browsing the shelves of the Kindle Store:

They're not looking for a lot of bells and whistles with their downloads—they simply want a good story, with no typos, at a decent price.

Good stories, no typos, decent price. That seems easy enough. But if it is that easy then how come so many Kindle publishers, both large and small, are filling the store with flubs that flop these days?

Simple. They're relying entirely on Amazon's Digital Text Platform to do their work for them, even though it's still in its infancy and has some significant flaws and bugs in the program. So, if these publishers don't bother to pre-format properly and then to proofread their "converted" documents before they hit the *publish* button—and evidently many of them don't— their finished products are a mess and, as far as the Kindle owners previewing them are concerned, completely unreadable. That means, even if such titles were written by famous authors, they're knocked right out of the competition, because nobody buys books they can't read, no matter who wrote them!

But, be it an essay, a short story or a novel, the bottom line is that it's easy to publish your writings for Kindle and to make them highly readable while you're at it, with very few customer returns and refunds as well. In fact, your manuscript can be uploaded and available for sale in the Kindle Store in just a matter of hours. IF YOU TAKE THE SHORTCUT…

OUTSTANDING IN THE FIELD
The Indie Author's Two-Step Guide to Publishing in the Kindle Store

The demand for producing this publishing guide for Kindle was to make it "short and sweet" so here goes:

Well, the experts said it would never happen but—oops—looks like they're wrong again! The day of the e-book has finally arrived via wireless-reader technology and Amazon wants you to help fill its Kindle catalogue and virtual bookshelves ASAP! So **log-in** right now with your Amazon customer name and password and go to their home-page menu options. From there, scroll down and click "Publishing With Kindle". The window that opens will be the Kindle Publishers' welcome page. If you click the log-in button to your left there, you'll see your publisher's account already set up and ready, and adding titles to it self-explanatory. (Note: You have to fill in your name, address, Social Security number and provide a valid U.S. bank account that Amazon can deposit your royalties into every month before you can actually hit that "publish" button! Sorry, no foreign accounts and no Paypal accounts will qualify at the moment.)

Once you have completed the required account info *and* saved it all, *and* presuming you have a manuscript in the form of an electronic document that you've proofread, edited, and then formatted so that each and every page of it looks like a book, *and* that you have a decent cover image to slap on it, then you're ready to upload and publish. It's just that simple.

YOU'RE NOT SURE? Okay, no problem. Let's check your materials list first. Here's the basic criteria and then some plain examples of how your e-doc file should appear if it's ready to upload to the Digital Text Platform for conversion and publishing. And since your cover images are also important, folks, (because they sell your books better!) you'll find some strict guidelines on image files and their sizes after that. Please do everything as outlined within this guide and you can be published in hours without encountering any serious obstacles.

FIRST THINGS FIRST: To use this shortcut your e-document must be saved as an ordinary *Microsoft/Word* Document and be completely pre-formatted. And, keeping in mind that you are not submitting your manuscript to a publisher, but that *you are the publisher,* your MS Word.doc must be pre-formatted to look very much like a book does, as enumerated below:

1. All the pages of your e-doc should be the same size and the margins, left to right, identical. (For instance, this guide was originally formatted in MS/ Word to 5.25" x 8" with .6" margins all around, which is similar to the dimensions of a Kindle. These specs are recommended because it makes it much easier to guess font sizes and placements, but you may choose any size you wish.)

2. Include a professional looking interior *title page with your name and book title on it. This should be the very first page and will be similar to the one in this tutorial, or to those you find in regular print books. Center everything you're putting on this page, making certain that you're centering with no paragraph indents. (Just click your 'Format' key on the MS/Word menu bar, then 'Paragraph', then 'Special' to check this. If correct, it should say 'None'.) Save.

*NOTE: If you want your cover image to appear before this page, as it does in our digital edition, consider that the Kindle cannot presently display it in color. If you want it there despite that shortcoming, then reduce your cover file considerably and "Save as" a brand new file, selecting the highest image quality available. (Important: inserting a tiny image of it will ensure it remains on the first page—if too large, it displaces it to the second page for some reason, and sometimes prevents your document from uploading at all. You may also convert to "grayscale" if you choose. Either way, make it tiny.) To insert the new cover image, click "Insert" on the MS/Word menu bar, scroll down to "picture" and select that file. Center absolute and save. You will also need to place a break beside or beneath the inserted image. If you don't know how to do page breaks yet, see number ten in this section. (Important: the conversion preview does not accurately show you what this image will look like in your Kindle book. Whether good or bad is a question of potluck!)

3. Single space your sentences. Double-spacing on a Kindle screen just looks wrong!

4. Don't get fancy with font styles or too large with them. Use a plain, readable 11 or 12 point font like Times New Roman for the text and chapter headings and you can't go wrong. (This guide used 12 point, Times New Roman.) If you've got complicated and large fonts, drop caps and the like, you'll see in your conversion preview window that Amazon's Digital Text Platform does not translate such details very well, so it's a waste of time to mess with them and, honestly, not that important.

5. Use indented paragraphs throughout. Just in case you don't know how to do this already, simply click 'Edit' on your MS/Word menu bar, then 'Select all' which will highlight the entire body of your text. Then click 'Special' again, but this time hit 'First line' and then pick the number of indent spaces you want. (Three is suggested.) Save.

6. Avoid paragraphs breaks. Let your indented paragraphs flow one right after another. This is attractive and will be the most readable. (DTP conversion might create way too much space between paragraphs, otherwise.)

7. *Justify the body of your text. Use 'Edit' and 'Select All' to highlight everything again and then locate the "Justify" button on the MS/Word menu bar. Click it. Save. (NOTE: If you are seeing too much spacing in your sentences, or you have concerns about text not flowing properly, then skip this design step. We simply feel that justified margins are more traditional, waste less space, and are more attractive overall.)

*UPDATE August 18, 2009: Good news! Recent improvements to the Digital Text Platform now enable you to achieve this same effect by simply aligning the margins of the body of your text to the left and then separately saving your MS Word.doc as an "RTF" Word document (click "Save as" and then select "Rich Text Format" from the drop down menu). The advantages of an RTF Word document extend beyond Kindle in that it allows your e-book text to freely "flow" on virtually all other electronic formats and e-reader devices currently available. Therefore we now highly recommend you use an RTF Word document for our shortcut so that you may easily publish it in other e-book stores as well as for the Kindle.

FYI: Stores such as Smashwords.com, Lulu.com, and Scribd.com, just to name a few, can easily covert the versatile Word doc and Word.rtf into MANY more appealing e-book styles than Kindle—and the more formats your book is converted into, the broader the audience and the better your sales!

8. Center all your headings or chapters (as is done throughout this guide) and place them at the very top of each new page with only one space between them and the opening paragraph. This will prevent too large a space appearing once they are converted.

9. Emphasize everything in advance. Meaning, if you want *italics*, **bold** fonts, or <u>underlines</u> to appear in the Kindle edition of your book they have to appear that way in your Word.doc first—DTP translates and converts these just fine.

10. Page breaks and section breaks must be formatted at the end of each chapter or new section in your Word/Doc. (If they're not, sometimes DTP converts your content into one big run-on.) To format breaks, click 'Insert' on the MS/Word menu bar and then 'Break'. For an ordinary page break just click 'Page Break' and for a whole section break click 'New Page'. Save. (Note: you do not need page breaks anywhere in your flowing content!)

MISCELLANEOUS: Don't even bother with page numbers because the Kindle wireless reader takes care of that on its own. Also, forget about designing headers and footers, too. They won't register right anyway and, frankly, they usually don't register at all. Ditto for a Table of Contents—most e-readers rely on "locations" or "percentages" instead of page numbers. Finally, interior illustrations throughout are really not recommended. For one, Kindle cannot replicate and display images in color as yet, and, two, many Kindle customers complain that even black and white image conversions and resolutions leave much to be desired.

OKAY, if your manuscript is formatted to all the above specifications it is, as they say in the business, "press-ready", which means you can e-publish this document *anyplace*. Just to be absolutely sure, though, take a glance at the next two pages following this section. They provide rough examples of what your e-doc title page and an interior page should look like. If your own formatting does in fact match these samples, good work! Click 'Save' on your MS/Word menu bar and then **upload** your document. (Note: if it takes longer than a half hour to achieve upload, cancel, close and then reopen the window, and then upload again. FYI: Continued problems with conversion indicates a defect in your file. Check it to make sure you haven't "embedded" fonts when you saved the document, or that your images aren't too large, etc. Adjust it as needed until the conversion finally takes.)

The section that follows these samples will discuss your book's cover and image file, so, if you're not an artist or graphic designer with a portfolio of work to choose from, start hunting through your albums or digital camera files for a good photo, because, having come this far, it would be a huge mistake if you didn't make a book cover. Books with cover images will typically outsell those without them, no matter how well-written the latter. (That's why the big publishing houses spend so much time and money on what they wrap their books in!)

one space
one space

THE GREAT AMERICAN NOVEL

by 22 Point Font

Times New Roman

2009

------insert page break here-----

.

Chapter One

---one space--

Text text text, text text, text text, text. Text text text text text. Text text text text *text* text text text text text text text. Text text text.

Text text text text. Text, text. Text text text… text. Text. Text text text, text text.

"Text, text text."

"Text?" Text text text text.

Text, text, text text. Text, text, text text text text text text *text* text text text text text text text text? Text, text text text text text text text text text text text. Text. Text, text text. Text text text text. Text, text text text.

"Text!"

----End of chapter. Insert your page break here---

A Cover For Your Kindle Book

Much can be said for a well-designed book cover, and much can be paid to procure one! The object, however, is to get your novel published and to do so quickly. And, of course to make you look good in the process. When your sales start coming in then you may want to seriously consider hiring a professional artist to redesign your cover for you. But, in the meantime, here are the rules regarding the image you plan on using right now:

1. The image you're about to upload is yours, or one to which you own the copyright or have been granted permission to use on your cover. Don't get off to a bad start here and find yourself sued. You stand to loose 100% of whatever you may earn from a copyright infringement, together with your reputation!

2. Your image is saved as an ordinary JPEG (or JPG) file, approximately 3" wide by 5" or so *but not smaller than 500 pixels on the longest side*, with a precise resolution of 300 dpi.

3. The title of your book and your name is clearly visible on this image. Whatever program you use to add text to your image, make certain that the type is crisp and clear and at least a quarter of an inch from the edges. That way, even if your photo is grainy or out of focus, it will come off as an intentional "design element" and make you look brilliant. (If you can't figure out how to add your text to the image, then just upload it without any. Something's better than nothing!)

4. The JPEG file name (and extension) contains only lowercase letters with no spaces between them. This is exceptionally important because DTP gets befuddled otherwise and will not accept your cover-file upload. In fact, there have been some cases where publishers remained stuck in the cover "uploading" mode indefinitely because of this little known bug in the system. To avoid that problem completely, here's an example of how to save your image file: *mybookcover.jpg* (That part of the file name *allinlowercaseletterswithnospaces*!)

5. If the cover uploading process takes longer than a half hour, cancel it and upload again. Lots of annoying things like this occur with DTP, but if your file is a JPEG, properly named, and sized right, then just cuss a little and start the upload again. If it happens more than once, however, then your JPEG image is simply too big. Reduce the size in increments, save, and repeat this and the upload process until it finally takes.

6. Once the thumbnail of your book cover appears on your screen click 'Save Entries'. If you forget to do this you'll lose your image and have to upload it again. Also, don't worry if the thumbnail preview seems kind of crappy. The actual "live" cover of your book will come out perfect.

So, if your cover image file meets the above specifications exactly—nice job—**upload it**! The next section provides a pre-publishing checklist. You should probably review it before clicking the DTP "Publish" button.

BEFORE YOU CLICK "PUBLISH"

1. Make sure you've completed all the "Product Details" for your e-book: title, author, publisher, a good description with no typos, a cover image, up to five relevant categories, the language it's written in, and all the appropriate keywords for Amazon's search engine. You can also insert the publishing date, too, or else just leave it blank and DTP will automatically do it for you. Leave blank the "ISBN" space as well, unless your e-book is also available in a print edition on Amazon. If it is, then include the ten digit ISBN (example: 1234567890) in the space provided and Amazon will link up both editions of it in their catalogue…eventually.

2. Check your conversion preview one last time to be certain there's no mistakes in your e-book. The preview window gives a very close approximation of how your content will appear on a Kindle. If you find a mistake, it likely originates in your MS/Word.doc, so you'll have to go back and fix it there, save all your changes, and then upload it once more for another conversion. (Aside from trashing the entire project and starting over again, there is no 'Delete" button for this - each upload replaces the last one you made.) Examine your new conversion preview and repeat the process as needed until you're satisfied with what you're seeing in the preview window.

3. The Price is Right! Be sure that the price is filled in and you're satisfied with it. Despite all the freebies floating around in the Kindle Store these days, the Indies are required to list their titles between .99 cents and $200. From that, Amazon then sets the final price, *discounting your book 0% to 100% as they see fit. You can make changes to your list price anytime, of course, but as for your initial MSRP (manufacturer's suggested retail price), it's your call as to what you think the item is worth. And, of course, your customers. *You'll find a few tips about pricing and other important things you should be aware of as a new Indie Publisher in the next section.

Oh, yes…go ahead now. Click **Publish!**

Congratulations You're Published!

SMOOTH OPERATOR
Bonus Tips and Tricks

Patience and persistence is essential for DTP Publishers because, despite the appearance of the "support" forums and an e-mail address (dtp-feedback@amazon.com) there's not actually any support for you in the truest sense of the word, and there aren't any phone numbers or DTP customer service reps, either. The following tips and tricks will point out the most common problems that Indies are experiencing and how best to approach and solve them independently. Consider this section your Indie survival guide.

1. *I published days ago, so why is the book just sitting on my dashboard shelf "ready" and not "live" yet?* The "save" button is your friend! At all aspects of the upload-to-publish process you must "save entries" and "save" the price and so on. That is to say, wherever you see a Save button, click it. When everything is uploaded and saved properly, a "publish" button will appear in the upper right of the window. You must click that button in order for your title to be published and go live. If you forget to, it'll just remain "ready" to publish forever.

2. *I clicked the "publish" button days ago and still have the message on my shelf that the book will be live in one to two hours...what's wrong?* This is the "stuck" mode that publishers find so exasperating. Usually, however, your title is "live", you just have to go search the Kindle Store to confirm this, a mission which might be like looking for a needle in a haystack, or then again maybe not, depending on if you're lucky. When you do finally locate your title and you discover you need to amend the listing, then e-mail "support" at the address above and tell them to get your book *un*stuck so you can make some corrections. (That'll probably take days on their part, and minutes off your life if you succumb to aggravation.) Otherwise, if your listing's perfect, or darn close to perfection, don't worry about the stuck-pubbing message. Eventually it will heal itself and a "live" link will properly appear on your shelf in its place.

3. *My book has gone "live" but where's the descriptive content?* It can often take days for your synopsis and other descriptions to appear on your new title's detail page, which is, unfortunately, the annoying norm. Sometimes, however, it doesn't ever appear, making it necessary to click the "feedback button" on your product's detail page and send Amazon notice of the problem. It's advisable to e-mail a follow-up message to "support" as well. (FYI: Whenever you don't get an answer from them and a problem still exists, it also never hurts to send an e-mail to: digitalrights@amazon.com. Although Amazon's Digital Rights department doesn't have much to do with the Indies except in cases of copyright infringements, and although they rarely answer and almost never politely, bugging them is bound to get you results sooner rather than later, no matter what the issue is.)

4. ***I made changes to my title days ago, why aren't they appearing on the detail page?*** Sometimes they won't! Use the e-mail addresses above when you've determined for a fact that this is the case.

5. ***I changed the price of my book and now the price with Amazon's discount added to it no longer makes any sense. What should I do?*** You must wait. Practically without fail the correct price with the discount will register on your detail page within twenty-four hours.

UPDATE 7/4/09 and 8/18/09: Amazon has ceased to apply discounts to the DTP Indie Publishers' new titles and has, in fact, stripped discounts from all of their earlier releases as well. This new policy is adversely affecting 100% percent of titles independently produced via the Digital Text Platform. Additionally, Amazon's pricing mechanism for the Indie titles appears to be "broken" as many DTP Publishers now report that attempts to lower their MSRP's have been foiled by the fact that Amazon won't budge the sell-at price...we will provide more details on this latest "snafu" as they come in but, in the interim, be sure to price your products low enough that you can compete against the majors' whose MSRP's are steadily climbing but whose discounts are nearly doubled now, bringing their prices low enough to compete against the more reasonable list prices of the Indies. (See Slate.com's July article for their insight on the e-book price-hiking scheme of mainstream publishers on Kindle.)

6. *I priced my book at .99 cents but there's no discount…why does everybody else have a discount but me?* [Update 7/4/09 and 8/18/09- See above #5]

7. *On a whim I just checked my account—where did my banking information go?* Don't check this on a whim, check your account information on a regular basis, say three or four times a month—at least! With frightening frequency, banking info somehow gets deleted from DTP Publishers' accounts and without this you can't get paid your royalties. Whenever you find that your valuable info is blank, just fill in the form again and SAVE. And be safe not sorry—repeat this procedure as often as necessary!

8. *According to my monthly "Transaction Report", I've made tons of sales, so why haven't I been paid yet?* For first-time publishers, usually this is because the full sixty days from the last day of the month that those sales were made in hasn't lapsed yet, and/or your sales haven't reached the minimum pay-out threshold of ten dollars. (But they will; so just be patient!) If, on the other hand, you've met both of this criteria and still haven't received your first wire transfer or check, and your banking info is up to date, then contact "support" immediately via the two e-mail addresses mentioned above. Thereafter, as long as you're earning ten dollars or more in royalties each month, you'll get regular royalty payments every thirty days. (March's sales at the end of May; April's at the end of June; May's at the end of July, etc.)

9. *What are all these returns in my transaction report?* Kindle Store customers are allowed to return a limited number of their digital purchases for a refund within seven days. Refunds are usually few and far between, though, so if you're finding a high return rate for one of your products, then check your customer reviews for feedback as to why, and if no reviews exist for it yet, then examine the files of that particular item yourself for sloppy formatting. If that's the problem, and it usually is, then correct your MS/Word.doc and just upload it again for conversion, as per the instructions in the first section of this guide.

10. *I can tell by my sales ranking/s that I'm selling, so why aren't those sales registering in my transaction report today?* This situation has happened to DTP Publishers more than once. Note: If your report is working properly then typically it will register the day's sales well before you see your sales rankings spike. In short, if sales aren't recording in relative sync with sales spikes for days on end, then there is a very serious problem that "support" needs to know about and fix. Use the e-mail addresses above to contact them and be persistent because, as with most Indie Publishers' issues, "support" is slow to react to this.

11. *I can tell by my transaction report that my book's been selling for weeks now, so why isn't there a sales rank on it?* Your book's being censored. But, never fear, this damage can be undone: re-categorize its listing and change some of your keywords. (Tips for avoiding the censor quicksand: If your book is for "grown-ups" it isn't necessarily "adult". Likewise, if you've written a romance that has love scenes in it, that doesn't make it "erotic/a". Finally, and until further notice, all writers in the "gay/lesbian" genre should assume a "don't ask, don't tell" stance when originally listing their titles on Amazon. After those titles are up and selling and a sales rank is posted on them, then add LGBT categories sparingly.)

12. *I just got a real crummy review from someone that I'm pretty sure is a competitor or an enemy, what can I do about it?* Some people are misery incarnate and, motivated by pure jealousy, will abuse the review feature in order to publicly post personal attacks and/or express rage at their own "quiet lives of desperation." Take heart in knowing that you can click 'Report this' to bring such a review to Amazon's attention, as well as vote it down as "unhelpful" with the 'No' button. Enlist your colleagues, friends, fans, and family to assist you in this endeavor and eventually the review will be expunged. Keep in mind, however, that the more reviews a book gets, even if they're bad, the higher that book will show in customer search results. Also realize that reviews of this nature tend to be banged out by howler monkeys on acid or crack and, as such, they're usually illiterate gibberish, or else so transparent that nobody pays any attention to them. In the end, it's up to you to decide how to handle an ugly review, but at least you can see that you do have some options.

13. *I can't download my "Transaction History Report" because it requires Excel, and/or my Excel program says it's an "invalid" file type and can't open it...what's going on here?* Amazon has steadily made changes to its DTP reporting system that have made it more and more opaque. Currently, there is no solution to this but an organized Indie revolt, which, by the sheer nature of being Independents, isn't likely to happen. Some publishers claim that they have successfully used other programs to open their history reports with. At present we at FREE PRESS can make no recommendations whatsoever as to which ones perform best and urge you, instead, to keep detailed records on your own, including any and all returns which are being deducted from your sales, in order to determine if your monthly royalty payments are accurate.

14. *I can open my history report okay, but why is it showing zero sales for last month when I know for a fact that plenty of sales were made?* With the new changes to the reporting system, there is also an accounting blackout period of almost one solid week, commencing from the last day of the most recent sales month through the very first week of the new one. During this time, all Indie Publishers' sales transactions for their past thirty days appear to equal zero! Again, there are no answers to this problem from Amazon and no solution in sight. But, if it's any comfort, your prior month's sales usually do "reappear" in about five to seven days. (But e-mail all over the place if they don't.)

15. *Why are there so many "freebies" from the major publishers in the Kindle Store of late, and how come they're on the bestselling lists?* A very popular question these days among the Indies:

Once upon a time, as a Kindle owner, those freebies were wonderful, but now, as an independent DTP Publisher whose sales are steadily being undermined by them, you feel they pose unfair competition to you and the representation of them as "best*sellers*", as well as their placement at the top of the Kindle "Best*seller*" lists, seems plainly deceptive. Worse, you hear that Amazon's paying the major publishers 35% to 50% royalties on their freebies if they have an MSRP listed on them, as most of them do. That's nice work if you can get it, you think, but you know that, as an Indie, <u>you can't</u>. So instead, you've marked your book way down to $1.00 and now Amazon is selling it for a measly .80 cents. That's improved sales a little bit and also helped to restore you to the ranks of a bestselling author again and, normally, you'd cheer about such an accomplishment, maybe even brag, but the nickels and dimes you're getting for that novel now hardly seem worth the effort because, you realize grimly, the bottom line is that, since your book isn't a freebie, you still can't adequately compete with it…

Welcome to the world of Indie publishing, where all the bases are loaded and so are the dice! Which is to say that you'll have to be very, very resourceful and innovative now in order to get—and keep—your Indie titles on the Kindle Store Bestseller lists.

To begin, be sure your target audience can readily find your book by cataloging it correctly and including all the appropriate keywords in its initial listing. After that, there are other things you should do for it and, while we can't say what methods will ultimately work best, we can direct you to those features and locations that, if utilized fully, will greatly improve your Kindle book's "discoverability" on Amazon, and your sales:

    a. Amazon customer reviews;
    b. Amazon tags;
    c. Amazon search suggestions;
    d. Amazon 'Listmania' lists;
    e. Amazon 'So-You'd-Like-To' lists;
    f. Amazon discussion forums.
    g. Your Amazon 'Author-Central' profile page;
    h. Your own website or blog;
    i. Social-networking sites (like Twitter);
    j. Other e-book retail sites (like Lulu)

Good luck, break-a-leg, and may the best Indie win!

from FREE PRESS Publications

IES WORKBOOK #3

BONUS Formatting Tips for Print Editions
A FREE GUIDE from Free Press

Thinking of releasing your popular e-book in a print edition, too?

Here's how…

QUICK-TIPS FOR PAPERBACKS
Bonus Formatting Tips for Print Editions

You can put a lot of design work into the interior of a paperback. Ours we kept fairly simple, but it still required a little expertise. This bonus section will provide you with the bare essentials for creating a pre-press book format of your electronic document. Just so you'll have an actual working example to refer to, we're going to describe how we formatted the very book you're holding right now in your hands, our *"Indie Empowerment Publishing Series"*. Please keep in mind that our book is 5" wide x 8" high. Your own book's final dimensions may be different.

The "raw" document we used was a Microsoft Word Document, set to "normal", "page layout":

1. Open your MS Word manuscript and click *FILE* on the tool bar;

2. Select *PAGE SET UP* from the drop-down menu;

3. From the pop-up window that appears next, select the *PAPER SIZE* tab; (enter *5"* for the width, *8"* for the height) and then click *PORTRAIT* for the paper orientation;

4. Now click the *MARGINS* tab and enter the following specs:

- 0.5" for the top/bottom/inside/outside margins;
- 0.4" for the "gutter" (for an average book);
- 0.3" for the "header";
- 0.4" for the "footer";
- "Mirror" margins (checkmark the box)

In the box that reads *APPLY TO,* select *"Whole"* document, after that click *OK*, and when the formatting box closes and the document fully changes to its new specifications and dimensions, then click *SAVE.*

Now, if all the pages of your manuscript suddenly appear off-center, then you did everything right! That extra 0.4" you see mirrored in the center there is for the manufacturing of the actual spine of the book, which when bound, eats up the inside edge of each page. This format you're looking at is a proper book publishing format. You, the publisher, can start embellishing it now—create your title and credit pages, center your chapter headings, justify your page margins, etc. You can also:

1.

Use the *FORMAT* key for designing classic drop-caps on each new chapter's opening paragraph (once inserted, just click them to tweak their sizes and positions). You can use this same key to indent your paragraphs, change your font styles, etc.;

2. Use the *VIEW* key to add your page footers and headers for customizing;

3. Use the *INSERT* key to add clip art and pictures, or to place the necessary page-break at the end of a chapter, or to create section-breaks for a new section and header (click "New Page" for that), or to add consecutive *page numbering to each new section, etc.;

*Page numbering got you a bit baffled? Yup, adding numbers can be a royal pain, but they're absolutely vital! We did ours by double-clicking each new footer in order to open it, then clicking INSERT on the MS Word toolbar, selecting CENTER from the pop-up menu, checking "Show Number on First Page", then clicking the additional FORMAT option there and filling in the precise (and accurate) number we wanted that page to "Start At". (Piece of cake.)

NOTE: Keep in mind that each actual page of a book is in fact two pages, front and back. This means that, whatever the final page count of your book is, <u>it must be an even number</u>. Each section of your book must likewise have an even number of pages in it. (New sections are added when you click INSERT and select "New Page". This also creates a brand new header and footer which you can keep the "Same as Previous" or modify accordingly.)

4. Use the *HELP* key on your MS toolbar to become your own master publisher!

Great. Everything's perfect. Now what are you supposed to do with this document?!

You have to convert your raw MS WORD.doc into a press-quality PDF (Portable Document Format) and then upload the PDF to your publisher's website for the printing and manufacturing of the final product—your book.

If you're familiar with PDF's and know how to create them with your own desktop application, just make sure this particular PDF you're making is not password protected and that it's set so it "embeds" all your fonts, images, clip art, etc. Some PDF programs have separate settings for embedding fonts and graphics while others simply allow you to request "press-quality". They're one and the same.

You can easily download a reliable PDF maker from *Adobe.com* to convert your final MS Word.doc yourself, or, even simpler, just upload it to a site that will give you the type of conversion required for book publishing.

FYI: As of the date of this publication, we're able to recommend *www.k2pdf.com* for both high quality, press-ready interior PDF's as well as for complete exterior wraparound book covers, too, so long as your cover image file doesn't exceed twenty-five (25) megabytes in size. (A full-color JPEG wraparound cover image of 300dpi for a standard 5.25" x 8" trade paperback is just under 25 MB and, as such, squeaks right by the limit.)

A wraparound book cover—what's that?!

Just as there is a back and a front to a page, so a book itself also has dimension: a front, a back, and a spine. Each of these sides must be perfectly designed and integrated to fit over your book's interior—to wrap around it. Here's the simple math of our 5" x 8" publication:

- front + back = 10.00" (width)
- add trim-edge   .25" (standard width)
- add spine   .26" (width)

Total trim width: 10.51"

- Height equals: 8.00"
- add trim-edge   .25" (standard)

Total trim height: 8.25"

FINAL COVER DIMENSIONS: 8.25" x 10.51"

You can add slightly more than the above standard quarter of an inch for the trim-edge all around, but it isn't necessary. Here's how you figure the width of your book's spine:

- white paper: number of pages x .002252
- off-white: number of pages x .0025
- color books: number of pages x .002347

Many of the do-it-yourself publishing platforms, like Amazon's *CreateSpace.com*, automatically calculate your spine width for you. All you have to do is open a free account with them, select the book dimensions and paper quality, enter the precise total number of pages, and then—ta dah—you've got the correct measurement. *CreateSpace* also offers a cover design template you can download, if you don't trust doing it all "freehand".

But if you are game to do it without assistance of any kind, then here are some basic design principles to follow:

- Only use images you have a right to use
- Keep all type .25" from the actual edges
- Bleed all your edges for ease of trimming
- Place the spine's type dead-center of layout

Concerning your book's International Standard Book Number (ISBN): Most POD publishing companies will assign this number to you when you register your title for production by them. It's a must have for listing your book with most retailers, whether they're brick-and-mortar operations or online sellers, or both.

And once you do get that ISBN, if you're designing the cover yourself, you will have to generate the barcode for it and then place this barcode in the lower right hand corner of the back of your book, similar to where ours is located.

ISBN 1438293461 −1

9 781438 293462 >

The bars in this image must be crisp and clean and, as to the size of the image itself, approximately 1.75" to 2.00" in width will work just fine. An excellent website for creating and downloading a workable barcode from your ten-digit ISBN is:

www.terryburton.co.uk/barcodewriter/generator

After you download it from them, remember to save the barcode in your design program so that you can easily lift it and *MOVE* it to your wraparound cover. You might also want to add a little more white space around the edges of it, just to insure trouble-free scanning at the checkout.

So that's it. Now you've got yourself a genuine paperback. You'll find that most of the marketing ideas in the first guide of this series will be the same for your hard-copy as for your e-book or Kindle edition. So just use your savvy, your wits, and that inimitable Indie spirit, and you'll start to go places with it. (And congrats again—good luck!)

If our publication has been informative and helped you to successfully publish and market a Kindle book or a paperback edition, or if there can be some improvements made to it, we ask that you post your comments, feedback and ratings in the form of a review on the website that you purchased it from. We look forward to hearing from you. And we thank you for purchasing this product!

We hope you found our guides useful.
You may also be interested in:

Interactive Directory

Coming Soon to Amazon Kindle
from
FREE PRESS Publications